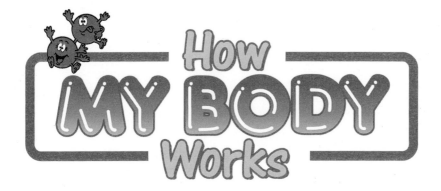

Leisure and Holidays

Leisure And Health

Time to relax

At the end of the last century, the working day was long and hard. It could last 14 hours or more and working conditions were often very bad and even dangerous. Even young children had to go out to work because they were expected to contribute to the family money. People would continue to work until illness or death put an end to their working life – there was no such thing as retirement for older people. This way of life is still common in many developing countries. In such circumstances physical

The Professor directs the body's defence system. He and Metro, his lieutenant, work to protect your body. Globus and his team of red blood cells need protection as they travel the body delivering oxygen. So Captain Courageous, chief of the white corpuscles and his friends Ace and Corpo cruise around the body attacking their enemies Virulus, the virus and Toxicus, the bacterium.

CONTENTS

and mental relaxation were almost impossible. It was only during the late 19th and early 20th centuries that workers succeeded in gradually improving conditions, working a shorter day with regular, public holidays (called **bank holidays**), and a longer holiday once a year as well.

In most developed countries the working day lasts about eight hours and people have about four weeks' holiday a year. This time off allows people to relax after working hard. When people are fully rested, they work better – their **productivity** is increased, which means that they produce more. Relaxation also protects their health.

At the beginning of this century, there was very little free time in the life of a working person. Now this has all changed and we have plenty of leisure time. We need to decide how to organise our free time so that we can relax and renew our energy levels. By doing these things, we keep ourselves mentally and physically fit.

Do you remember?

The kidneys, cleaning blood

The main job of the kidneys is to clean the blood. They also produce a yellowish liquid called urine. The kidneys send urine to the bladder through two narrow tubes called ureters. The urine then passes out of the body via the urethra.

The kidneys contain about a million mini-kidneys each called **nephrons**. These **filter** out waste substances and water from the blood.

The body needs a constant amount of water. It gets its water from solid and liquid foods, and from drinking. This water is passed out through the skin as sweat, or through the kidneys and then the bladder as urine. The kidneys produce more or less urine depending on how much water is in the body at the time. In this way, the water in the body is kept at the correct level.

THE PARTS OF THE KIDNEY

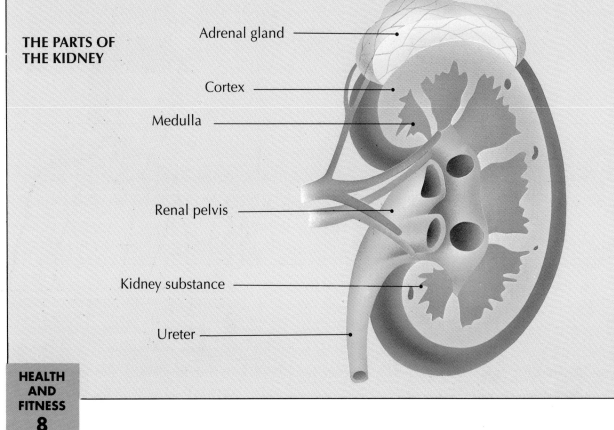

Adrenal gland

Cortex

Medulla

Renal pelvis

Kidney substance

Ureter

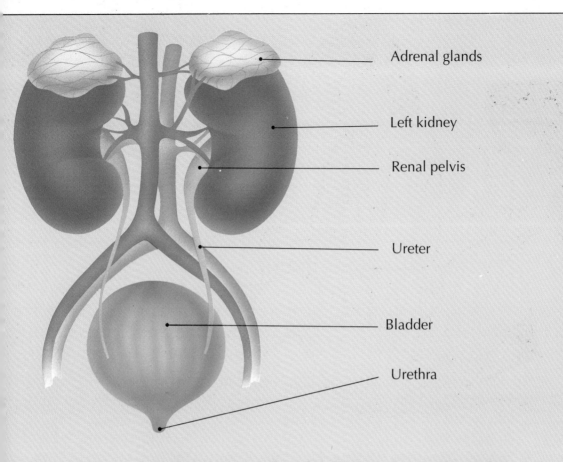

Adrenal glands

Left kidney

Renal pelvis

Ureter

Bladder

Urethra

What are the kidneys made of?

The kidneys are shaped like a bean and are 10cm to 12cm in length. They sit on either side of the spine. The adrenal glands (sometimes called the supra-renal glands), which produce hormones, are at the upper end of each kidney. The kidneys are made up of the following parts:

● the renal capsule, a tough fibrous skin wrapped around the kidneys which protects them.

● the cortex where urine production starts.

● the medulla which links the cortex to the centre of the kidney.

● the renal pelvis, the funnel-shaped inner part of the kidney. This is where the urine collects before it is passed to the bladder.

The kidneys clean approximately 1,800 litres of blood every day and produce one and a half litres of urine as a result. The urine passes through the ureter to the bladder, which is like a balloon with muscles. It expands as it fills with urine and contracts when you go to the toilet, pushing the urine out of the urethra.

Get active

All too often leisure is confused with doing nothing. Time when a person is not working or learning may be spent in idleness. As a result, people become lazy and believe there is nothing new to discover about the world. These people, sooner or later, become bored with life.

A person who works eight hours every day has 16 hours of free time. Only half of these hours are needed for eating and sleeping, so what to do with the rest of the time is a matter of choice. Some people may spend the time with family or friends, going out to the theatre or to a restaurant, reading a good book, visiting an exhibition or seeing a film – to give just a few examples.

Weekends are a good time for organising outings and short expeditions. When planning these trips, avoid stressful conditions. A walk in the country or a visit to the seaside are great fun, but if you have to spend two hours in heavy traffic to get there you will not end up feeling very relaxed. Think carefully when deciding how to spend your leisure time.

After a hard drive in bad traffic the man on the beach is finding it very hard to relax – especially when he knows he may have the same problems going home.

ALL WORK AND NO PLAY

In days gone by, there were no holidays. Ordinary people used to work all year round, except for certain religious holidays which gave people a brief rest from their hard life. However, if you were lucky enough to live at court, it was very different. For centuries, kings and queens, lords and ladies used to take advantage of ordinary working people, making them pay taxes on their small earnings. Sometimes these taxes were paid with money, and other times with things the people had made or grown.

There were many riots and revolts by **peasants**, as the poor country people were called, but they had no way of changing their lot. It was a long time before the old systems of government altered and a new **social order** was allowed to develop. Only during the late 19th century did far-reaching changes in working conditions take place as a result of the workers themselves complaining to their governments.

Holidays

Holidays forever!

Regular holidays, that everyone is entitled to take, are now a matter of course in the developed countries of the world. In these countries, all workers have the opportunity of doing whatever they like for a few weeks in the year. They may like just to stay at home and enjoy one of their hobbies. They may want to travel abroad, especially if they have friends and relations in other countries. When on holiday, we can give the body and mind a chance to recharge their energy levels, spend time with family and friends, practise some sport, read, write, draw, paint and, of course, relax.

Holidays are meant to refresh both the body and the mind. We leave our everyday world behind and can get to know new people and widen our horizons. Common interests bring people together and everyone returns home with many happy memories.

Where shall we go?

If you are in good health, there is an endless choice of places to go on holiday. But don't forget that you are used to your own climate, and a sudden

change for a short while may not be too good for you. This is especially true if you have any health problems.
Take a few precautions to ensure you are fit enough to enjoy your holiday to the full.
● Pay special attention to personal hygiene.
● Always check that food is fresh and edible and that water is fit to drink.
● Even if you love getting a tan, never go out in the sun without protection or sunbathe for too long.
● Take the right clothes and footwear for the weather and the countryside of the country you are visiting.
● You may like sport, but do not underestimate the difference in climate or overestimate your own strength.

This young boy can really enjoy his holidays. He is having great fun fishing and wears a T-shirt to protect himself from the sun, so there is no danger of his holidays being spoilt by sunburn.

First aid kit for travelling

Y ou should always pack a first aid kit when going away, regardless of where you are spending your holidays – in the countryside or at the seaside, in your own country or abroad.

Include the following in your first aid kit for travelling:
- A small book of first aid instructions – this is especially useful if you are travelling to a country where you do not speak the language as you may find it difficult to understand advice
- Bandages and dressings, including gauze and absorbent cotton wool
- Adhesive dressings and plasters
- Small scissors
- Tweezers to remove thorns and splinters

- Disinfectant and antiseptic solution or cream
- Antihistamine cream for stings
- Medication to stop severe diarrhoea
- Painkillers
- Travel-sickness or sea-sickness pills, if necessary
- Indigestion tablets for upset stomachs
- Sun lotion or sun cream to protect you from sunburn
- An insect repellent cream
- Eye drops for irritation caused by strong sun or chlorine in a swimming pool

A scratch, a cut, an insect bite or a small burn are usually not serious if you travel with a well-equipped first aid kit. The same is true of car-sickness and sea-sickness, headache and indigestion. Be well prepared and make the most of your holiday time.

GAUZE

iseptic

Here comes summer

In summer people tend to spend more time out in the open, enjoying the warmth of the sun and swimming in the sea or in a swimming pool. Many people take their holidays in the summer and choose seaside resorts or a place near a lake. You can also enjoy all kinds of outdoor sports when the weather is good, such as golf, tennis and basketball. Many people love the water, which explains why beaches can be so overcrowded in summer. Sometimes it seems impossible to find even the tiniest place on a good beach, but once settled, there is no shortage of things to do and new friends to play with.

Although human beings are not designed to live in the water, many are strongly attracted to it. Even small babies love to splash in the water and children have a wonderful time in the waves. A day on the beach is always great fun for the whole family, and swimming is very good for your health. However, don't forget that swimming can also be dangerous. You need to follow a few safety rules so that your holiday is not spoilt by an accident.

The beach is a wonderful place for building sand castles or playing ball. You can lie in the sun, read a good book or the newspaper and have a dip now and again to refresh yourself. Many people think this is a perfect holiday. However, both the water and the sun can be dangerous. Read the advice in the following pages for an accident-free time.

How annoying! The weather forecast says there will be bad weather all day. Thunder clouds are approaching and a storm is brewing. When there is a storm warning, you must never go swimming or set out to sea. This boy is very disappointed at first because he will not be able to go the beach and swim. However, it is better to be safe than sorry. The person on the beach has ignored the storm warning. You can see what problems he is having. There are strong winds, the sea is very rough and the enormous waves are very threatening. On holiday expect some days of bad weather. Take a board game, a good book and find out what museums and art galleries there are to visit near your holiday home.

Be wise!

To enjoy swimming and to avoid accidents, you must observe the following rules at all times:

● Never go into the water with a full stomach or when you are very hot. Do not swim if you feel tired, faint, have earache or are unwell.

● Only experienced, strong swimmers should swim out of their depth or far from the shore.

● If there is a red flag flying at the beach it means that it is dangerous to swim and on no account should you enter the water.

Never swim on a full stomach as you may get stomach cramp which will prevent you from swimming to safety. Allow yourself an hour or so after eating, before going in the water.

● Do not jump into cold water without first cooling down. If your body temperature is very hot, perhaps from playing a game in the sun, the sudden coldness of the water can cause you to pass out.

● Very small children who cannot swim must be watched at all times when they are on the beach. In just seconds they can fall into danger.

● If you can swim, you have no need to fear the water, but do not underestimate possible dangers or overestimate your own strength. Water, whether the sea, lakes or rivers, should always be treated with great respect.

● People who go sailing and windsurfing must always listen to the weather forecast and should not go out if bad weather is expected.

Swimming pool safety

There are several kinds of swimming pools. As well as indoor and outdoor pools designed for fun and pleasure, there are pools for competitive swimming and diving, therapeutic treatment or water gymnastics. In all pools very strict rules of hygiene must be observed because so many people use the water.

Every swimming pool must be equipped with changing rooms, showers, lavatories and a foot bath. It is essential to shower and walk through the footbath before and after using the pool to help stop the spread of germs.

Swimming pools must also have a first aid station and trained lifeguards.

Disinfectants containing chlorine are usually added to the water to kill any germs that get into it from the many bodies that use the pool. Do not use a swimming pool if you have an infection or feel under the weather. Your germs may be passed on to others, and you will be more likely to pick up germs yourself in the water. A good hot shower, drying your body and your hair thoroughly and then having a hot drink when you come out will normally prevent you from getting ill as a result of swimming.

Virulus and other germs like him don't stand a chance of survival in this swimming pool. The water is protected with a disinfectant and the children are being careful to shower and dry off well after swimming.

Air travel

Many people like going on holiday abroad. Travelling by plane is marvellous – you can cover long distances in a very short time, and flying is a very safe, efficient way of travelling. However, to feel well during a long flight and alert when you arrive, the following rules will help you:

● If you suddenly feel that your ears have become blocked and you cannot hear properly, do not worry. In a plane you sit in a **pressurised** cabin, where the air pressure is controlled. The

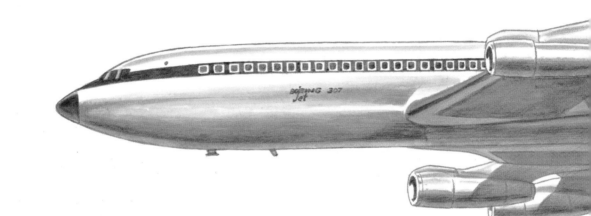

On all passenger flights travellers are looked after by stewards and stewardesses whose task it is to make the passengers' journey as pleasant as possible. They know exactly what you should do at all times during the flight.

They will give you a drink and, very often, something to eat. There may be a film to watch, or some music to listen to through headphones. If you feel unsure about anything, ask the stewardess to explain it to you.

pressure in the ear changes when the plane goes up or comes down, and this can make you deaf for a short time. You can clear your ears by swallowing or yawning, and it is a good idea to chew on a sweet when taking off or landing. Small babies can suck on a bottle or dummy to keep their ears clear.

● Drink plenty of water and fruit juice because the air in the plane is dry and your body may become **dehydrated** – dried out – on a long journey.

● Avoid fizzy drinks and heavy meals. The changes in pressure in the plane can lead to digestive upsets, so do not overload your stomach.

● On a long flight you may find you suffer from **jet-lag**. On a long journey people often get confused about the time – considering when you left home, you may think it is bedtime when you arrive at your destination. However, it may be

only lunchtime. This time confusion can make you feel very, very tired. Get plenty of sleep on the plane, eat and drink a little and often, and try to keep awake until it is night time where you have landed rather than going to sleep when you feel like it. Have a great time and you will forget about jet-lag.

● If you suffer from air sickness, suck a sweet or chew some gum, and find something interesting to take your mind off being in the plane. Play a game, or, on a longer flight, you may be able to watch a film.

● Some people feel afraid of flying. If this is the case with you, find out as much as possible about how the plane works and ask if you can go on the flight deck and see the pilot. Flying is a very safe form of travel and it is often the rather strange noises and weird feelings caused by the way the aircraft moves, that make people frightened. If you understand these, you are less likely to be afraid. Remember, you are more likely to have an accident driving in a car on the way to the airport than in the air.

Travelling by car

Although cars pollute the environment, they are a very convenient method of transport. A car lets you go straight to your destination without having to wait for flights or trains. You can take more luggage than if you travel by plane or train, and when you arrive, you can use the car to get around.

Sadly, there are still many accidents on the roads. Before any long journey the car should be checked and serviced. There is nothing worse than breaking down in a foreign country, especially when you know the problem could have been solved by a repair before the journey started. The driver must find out about the motor regulations in the countries being visited and may need to fit adjusters to the headlights and display a nationality sticker. Often, special insurance is required.

Make sure the car has a first aid kit, a fire extinguisher, and the necessary equipment for changing tyres and carrying out minor repairs.

Driving on foreign roads and finding the way can be very hard work for the driver. The passengers must not distract him or her, and all people in the car must be strapped in with seat belts and not fidget around. Small children must be securely strapped in child seats and babies in safe baby seats.

It is important to take regular breaks when travelling, so that everyone can stretch their legs and get some fresh air. Drivers must stop if they feel that they can no longer concentrate. If this happens, a break is needed, or another driver must take over.

Many accidents and breakdowns could be prevented if drivers behaved in a more responsible manner. Regular car maintenance is very important, along with paying careful attention to the road conditions.

CAMPING

Living and sleeping in a tent or a caravan on a camp site is great fun. It is an excellent way of spending holidays and is not expensive. There are very good camp sites all over the world, with good facilities. Some are near the coast, others in the countryside or in the mountains. Living in a tent for a couple of weeks is a complete change from everyday life.

When camping, everyone has to join in with the cooking, washing-up and keeping the site clean and tidy. It is a good family holiday and many day-to-day activities, such as making breakfast, seem much more exciting under canvas.

There are many rules and regulations on camp sites that everyone must abide by, and you must only camp on proper sites and not on the open road or in the countryside. Camping is a great way to 'get back to nature'.

KEEPING FIT

● Rugby

Rugby was invented in 1823 at Rugby School in England, and soon spread to other schools. The new winter sport quickly became very popular and by the middle of the 19th century the first rugby club had been founded; soon there were clubs in France, Australia, New Zealand and South Africa. Rugby now has many well-known teams with a great number of followers.

Rugby has the reputation of being a rough sport, but statistics show that the risk of serious injuries is relatively low compared with football. Its reputation as a violent sport is based on the way the players tackle their opponent when they are trying to get the ball. This often looks more dangerous than it really is, and the referee carefully controls how tough the action can be. In reality, this team sport promotes fairness, loyalty and self-control in its players.

The game is played with an oval ball about 28cm long. The playing field is 68-70 metres wide and about

This player is attempting a conversion. To do this the ball must be kicked over the 3m-high crossbar linking the two goal posts, which are placed 5.64m apart. The conversion adds two extra points to the three already scored with the try.

Two teams are in a scrum, trying to get possession of the ball. In a scrum the players are not allowed to touch the ball with their hands.

100 metres long. At each end there is a try line with a goal in the middle of it. A team is made up of 15 people. They are allowed to handle the ball, as well as kick it, and the object is to score as many points as possible during the game which is 80 minutes long for seniors and 60 minutes long for juniors. This is achieved by getting the ball over the opponent's try line and touching it down on the ground; this is called a try. A try can be converted into a goal (worth more points) by kicking the ball over the crossbar of the goal posts. At certain times during the match the players also form scrums, when they lock together and try to kick the ball out from below them to one of their players outside who is waiting for it.

Rugby players need to be able to run very fast, be quick-witted to avoid the opposition who will be attempting to tackle them, and not worried about a bruise or two. There are several important international matches each year, which involve teams travelling abroad. For example, the All Blacks from New Zealand travel to Britain to play Scotland, England and Wales.

Many schools play rugby as well as football, and most towns have a local team. If you enjoy sport, rugby can be great fun and a good winter activity.

KEY WORDS

Antihistamine – medicine for the treatment of allergies.

Antiseptic – a germ-killing substance, especially used when dealing with wounds.

Dehydrated – with all its moisture removed, dried-out.

Filter – to remove particles from a water or gas by passing it through a substance that traps the particles.

Jet-lag – great tiredness that someone feels after a long air journey because he or she has not got used to the time differences in different parts of the world.

Peasant – an historical word for a person who worked on the land and who may have been very poor.

Pressurised – kept at a constant air pressure.

Productivity – the amount that someone produces.

Social order – the way in which a community organises itself.

HOW MY BODY WORKS

HOW MY BODY WORKS is an educational series that builds into a complete encyclopedia of the human body. Each volume introduces and explains one of its mysteries.

In Part 49 of How My Body Works you've found out how much we need leisure time and holidays so that we feel well.

Part 50 is the last volume of the series. It will contain a full index so that you can look up any subject you need in your collection. In this way, you will find **How My Body Works** even more useful in school and project work.

Albert Barillé (pictured left) is the author of this fascinating series of books. The human body is a series of complex systems and mechanisms, so to make it easier for you to understand how the body works, Barillé created The Professor, Captain Courageous, Globus, Toxicus and Virulus, plus many other colourful cartoon characters, to show you around. The Professor and his friends guide you through the body, explaining how it works in a clear and simple way that makes it fun.

TEST YOUR KNOWLEDGE
The Leisure and Holidays Quiz

More than one answer may be correct

1. How long is an average working day?
a) about 4 hours
b) about 8 hours
c) about 24 hours

2. What are bank holidays?
a) regular, public holidays
b) a day when adults all go to the bank
c) a national fishing day

3. What is the main job of the kidneys?
a) pumping blood around the body
b) putting oxygen into the blood
c) cleaning the blood

4. How many kidneys are there in the body?
a) two
b) four
c) twenty

5. How many litres of blood does the kidney clean each day?
a) 180 litres
b) 1,800 litres
c) 18,000 litres

6. What do you carry in a first aid kit for travelling?
a) small scissors
b) a jack for mending a car puncture
c) tweezers

7. When should you not go swimming?
a) if there is a storm warning
b) if there is a red flag flying at the beach
c) if you have just eaten a large meal

8. How are swimming pools kept clean?
a) by all swimmers using a footbath
b) by adding washing up liquid to the water
c) by adding disinfectant to the water

9. What should you drink on a long flight?
a) water
b) fruit juice
c) fizzy drinks

10. What must a driver do before taking a car abroad on holiday?
a) have the car serviced
b) check that the car insurance is correct
c) find out about the driving regulations in the country being visited

ANSWERS to the **'How My Body Works'** Leisure and Holidays Quiz are in Issue 50.
Answers to Issue 48
1 (c), 2 (c), 3 (b), 4 (a), 5 (b), 6 (c), 7 (a), 8 (b), 9 (a & c), 10 (b)

Published by
ORBIS PUBLISHING,
Griffin House,
161 Hammersmith Road,
London W6 8SD

BACK ISSUES
Back issues can be obtained by placing an order with your newsagent or, in case of difficulty, from our back numbers department. All cheques/postal orders should be made payable to Orbis Publishing Ltd.

BACK ISSUE CHARGES
Volume 1:
UK: 99p plus £1.00 p&p;
Eire: IR£0.99 plus £1.00 p&p
Thereafter:
UK: £2.99 plus 50p p&p;
Eire: IR£3.50 plus 50p p&p

ADDRESS FOR
BACK ISSUES:
Orbis Publishing Ltd, Unit 10, Wheel Lane Business Park, Wheel Lane, Westfield, Hastings, East Sussex, TN35 4SG. Tel: 0424 755755

BACK ISSUES OVERSEAS
Please place requests for copies of back issues with your newsagent or, in case of difficulty, please write to the relevant address given:

Australia
Gordon and Gotch Ltd, PO Box 290, Burwood VIC 3125 (Enclose cover price plus $1 p&h per issue)

New Zealand
Gordon and Gotch (NZ) Ltd, PO Box 584, Auckland.

South Africa
Back issues Dept Republican News Agency PO Box 16034 Doornfontein 2028

Malta & Singapore
Back numbers are available at LM1.50 from your newsagent.

© Procidis Albert Barillé
© 1994 Orbis Publishing Ltd, London
N49 94 07 21
ISBN 0 7489 1046 8
Printed in Italy by Officine Grafiche De Agostini, Novara